SO-ART-844

CHALLENGING
Critical
Thinking
PUZZLES

Michael A. DiSpezio
Illustrated by Myron Miller

Sterling Publishing Co., Inc.
New York

Library of Congress Cataloging-in-Publication Data

DiSpezio, Michael A.
    Challenging critical thinking puzzles / by Michael A.
DiSpezio ; illustrated by Myron Miller.
        p.   cm.
    Includes index.
    ISBN 0-8069-3186-8
    1. Puzzles. 2. Critical thinking. I. Miller, Myron, 1948– .
II. Title.
GV1493.D53   1998
793.73–dc21   98-6167
                                                                    CIP

10 9 8 7

Published by Sterling Publishing Co., Inc.
387 Park Avenue South, New York, NY 10016
© 1998 by Michael A. DiSpezio
Distributed in Canada by Sterling Publishing
c/o Canadian Manda Group, 165 Dufferin Street,
Toronto, Ontario, Canada M6K 3H6
Distributed in Great Britain by Chrysalis Books Group PLC
The Chrysalis Building, Bramley Road, London, W10 6SP, England
Distributed in Australia by Capricorn Link (Australia) Pty. Ltd.
P.O. Box 704, Windsor, NSW 2756, Australia

Manufactured in the United States of America
All rights reserved

Sterling ISBN 0-8069-3186-8

For information about custom editions, special sales, premium and
corporate purchases, please contact Sterling Special Sales
Department at 800-805-5489 or specialsales@sterlingpub.com.

CONTENTS

✦ ✦ ✦

Acknowledgments

Once more, I have had the enjoyable opportunity to work with a sterling team on this, the third book in a set of *Critical Thinking Puzzles*. Without each member's talent, support, and untiring eye for catching my oversights, publications such as this would not be possible. Therefore, I'd like to acknowledge the dedication and constant upbeat attitude of my editor Hazel Chan and artist Myron Miller. They have succeeded in nurturing this puzzle series. I'd also like to recognize Sheila Barry for her continual support, encouragement, and insight into the project's creation and success.

INTRODUCTION

Data, data, and more data. We live in an age when the acquisition and presentation of new knowledge and information is astonishing. From the Internet to CD libraries, new technologies generate the means by which information transfer attains extraordinary dimension. Even when one considers the ability for "good old" print to disseminate knowledge, its capacity is no less than remarkable. Consider this: It is said that the present Sunday edition of the *New York Times* contains more information than the average person living in the 1800s would encounter in a lifetime!

Since the access and acquisition of new knowledge continues to expand, we must learn how to cope with this information overload. We need to develop and nurture thinking skills and strategies that will help us examine, evaluate, and apply new knowledge in a fair-minded manner. That's where critical thinking skills come in.

Although some educators and psychologists use the term "critical thinking" broadly by applying it to a range of thinking abilities, most restrict the use of it to specific strategies that help us better interpret and apply facts. These strategies include skills such as: predicting, making accurate observations, generalizing, comparing and contrasting, uncovering assumptions, understanding connections, reasoning through analogies, and finding causes.

Educators and psychologists don't agree on the most effective way to develop these skills. Some feel that they should be taught independent of any content, such as real-life situations. This way the strategies are not confused or compromised with the importance of content. As a result, critical thinking skills can be more effectively considered as independent tools that can be applied to a range of circumstances.

Other experts, however, think that content is essential to teaching critical thinking skills. By utilizing real-life situations, students may then appreciate the value of these skills in the analysis of facts. This combination forms an intricate network of connections that produce a deeper understanding of content while offering a thinking platform from which to analyze additional situations.

It is with the latter approach in mind that this book was put together. It uses mind-bending puzzles as an arena to practice critical thinking skills. As you'll discover, this isn't a textbook or a bulletin on critical thinking. (For that type of reference, you'll need to check out a university library.) Instead, this puzzle book, as in the previous two of this series, offers both new puzzles and traditional puzzles with a contemporary twist. All of them are brain-busting challenges that guarantee to engage a battery of your critical thinking skills. So hang on to those brain cells, because here we go again!

—Michael

THE PUZZLES

Puzzle Paths

Sam Loyd was one of the most published and brilliant puzzle creators of all time. Born in 1841, Sam was an accomplished chess player by his early teens. He created puzzles based upon the moves of chess pieces. Loyd also produced thousands of other puzzles, many of which still appear today with contemporary twists and slight modifications. The maze below is based upon one of his earliest puzzle ideas. Can you complete the challenge?

The *Amusing Amusement Park* has three rides. It also has three gates with signs that identify the ride to which they lead. The only problem is that the architect forgot the layout of the connecting paths. Can you help? Draw three paths that connect the rides to their gates. The paths can't meet or cross.

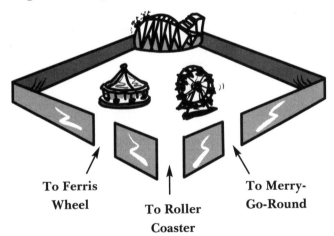

To Ferris Wheel

To Roller Coaster

To Merry-Go-Round

Answer on page 84.

Turn, Turn, Turn

◆ ◆ ◆

Ever heard of a multiaxial stimulator? Years ago, it appeared as a training device for astronauts and pilots. Nowadays, it's often found at beaches, amusement parks, and fairs. The MAS consists of three loops, each inside of the other. Each loop is free to rotate in only one dimension. The "pilot" is fastened to the middle of the innermost loop. In this position, a person gets to experience all three turning motions at the same time.

Let's strap the number "4" in this simulator. Suppose each of the loops made one half rotation. How would the "4" appear after it was flipped, turned, and spun halfway in all three dimensions? You can select from the choices below.

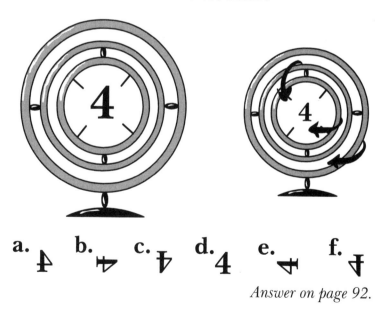

a. b. c. d. e. f.

Answer on page 92.

Mind Bend

According to Einstein, in some places the shortest distance between two points is not a straight line! Consider this: In space, the gravitational field of huge objects is strong enough to warp space. In these curved dimensions, the concept represented by a straight line bends to fit the framework of the distorted space. Mind bending, huh?

Here's another type of mind bender. The shape below is made from a single index card. No section of the card has been removed or taped back in place. Can you duplicate its appearance using several snips of a scissors? Have fun!

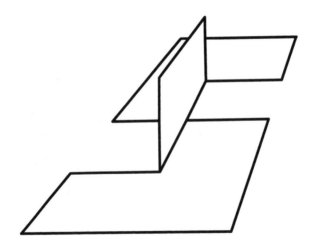

Answer on page 81.

Whale of a Problem

In spite of their name, killer whales don't hunt and kill people. In fact, these dolphin-like animals prefer to eat smaller marine animals, such as seals and penguins. Biologists believe that rare attacks on humans occur because of misidentification. Obscured by daylight or icebergs, the image of a person may be mistaken for that of a penguin from below.

Now here's the problem. Acting alone, it takes two killer whales 2 minutes to catch two seals. Based upon this rate, how long will it take a pod of ten killer whales to catch ten seals?

Answer on page 93.

Main Attraction

✦ ✦ ✦

Like all magnets, a bar magnet has a North and South Pole. At each of these poles, the magnetic force is the strongest. It is powerful enough to attract and repel iron objects. Near the middle of the magnet, however, the force is hardly detectable.

Suppose you have two identical iron bars. Only one of the bars has been magnetized. Suppose you can only pick up and manipulate one bar of these two bars. How can you tell if it is the magnetized or unmagnetized bar?

Answer on page 80.

Runaway Runway

✦ ✦ ✦

"Good afternoon. This is your captain speaking. We're fourth in line for departure. As soon as these four albatross birds take off, we'll begin our flight. Thank you for your patience."

Strange, but true. Pilots must sometimes compete with birds for runway usage. The same physical principles that lift an aircraft into the sky are at work in our feathered friends. Runways that are constructed to offer better lifting conditions for aircrafts inadvertently produce great takeoff locations for birds.

Speaking of runways, here's our puzzle. If an airport has three separate runways, there can be a maximum of three intersections. Suppose there are four runways. What is the maximum number of possible intersections?

Answer on page 85.

Raises and Cuts

✦ ✦ ✦

Like many modern-day products, paper toweling arose from a factory mistake. A mill-sized roll of paper that should have been cut and packaged into soft bathroom tissue was manufactured thick and wrinkled. Instead of junking the roll, the workers perforated the unattractive paper into towel-sized sheets. And so, the paper towel was born.

Several years ago, Moe and Bo began work at a paper towel factory. At the end of the first week, the owner evaluated both workers. Pleased with Moe, she increased his weekly wage by 10%. Disappointed with Bo, she cut her salary by 10%. The following week, the owner decided to make their salaries more equal. To do so, she cut Moe's new salary by 10%. At the same time, she increased Bo's salary by 10%. Now, which worker earned more?

Answer on page 85.

The Race Is On

The material we call rubber is another product of a mishap in the kitchen! Prior to the mid-1800s, rubber was a troublesome material. In the summer heat, it became soft and sticky. In the winter cold, it became hard and brittle. In searching for a way to improve the properties of rubber, Charles Goodyear accidentally spilled a spoonful of a rubber and sulfur mixture onto his stove. When he later examined the solidified spill, he uncovered a flexible material that could withstand heat and cold.

Take a look at the two solid rubber wheels below. Both have been modified by retired ice skaters. On the first wheel, 4 pounds of lead are positioned in one central lump. On the second wheel, the same amount of lead is spread out into four 1-pound lumps so that they are positioned closer to the wheel's rim.

Suppose these wheels are released down identical inclines. If we don't consider air resistance, will these wheels accelerate at the same rate?

Answer on page 88.

Screwy Stuff

♦ ♦ ♦

Take a close look at the two screws below. Suppose they were both turned in a counterclockwise rotation. What will happen to each screw?

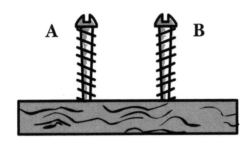

Answer on page 87.

Screws in the Head

♦ ♦ ♦

The pitch made by a vibrating string is dependent upon several factors, including the tension in the string. The more tightly pulled (greater tension), the higher the pitch. Likewise, if the string is relaxed (less tension), it produces a note of lower pitch.

Many guitars have a screw-like arrangement that varies the tension in the individual strings. As the tuner head is turned, this movement is transferred to a post. The turn of the post changes the tension in its wrapped string to produce a note of different pitch.

Take a look at the tuning heads below. What happens to the pitch of the sound when the head is rotated in a clockwise manner?

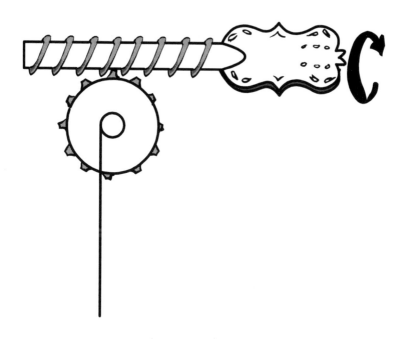

Answer on page 87.

Change of Pace

✦ ✦ ✦

Here are several puzzles that use a handful of change.

Consider this: I have ten coins in my pocket. The value of these coins is 50 cents. How many coins of each denomination are there?

Okay, so that one wasn't too difficult. How about finding the identity of thirty coins whose value is $1.00?

Answer on page 72.

Spiral²

♦ ♦ ♦

While exploring the ruins of an ancient city, an archaeologist uncovers an odd structure. The structure is made of stone walls that form a square spiral. The sides of the outside spiral measure 100 feet × 100 feet. The path throughout the entire structure is 2 feet wide.

If the archeologist walks along the exact center of the path, how far will he travel from the entrance to the end of the spiral?

Answer on page 88.

Take 'em Away

This arrangement of toothpicks forms fourteen different squares of various sizes. Can you remove six toothpicks and leave only three squares behind?

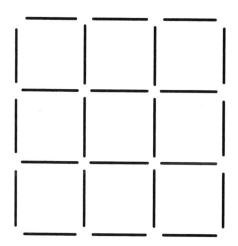

Answer on page 90.

Don't Stop Now

Now that you are familiar with the pattern, let's try one more removal problem. Starting with the same twenty-four toothpick grid, remove eight toothpicks and leave exactly three squares behind.

Answer on page 74.

Get Set. Go!

✦ ✦ ✦

Two cyclists race along a straight course. The faster of the pair maintains an average speed of 30 mph. The slower cyclist averages 25 miles per hour. When the race ends, the judges announce that the faster cyclist crossed the finish line one hour before the slower racer. How many miles long was the racing course?

Answer on pages 75–76.

Coin Roll

✦ ✦ ✦

Run your fingernail around the rim of a dime or quarter and you'll feel a series of small ridges. These ridges appeared on coins hundreds of years ago. At that time, many coins were made out of silver and other valuable metals. To prevent people from "shaving" the metal from the edge of the coin (and selling the metal shavings), telltale ridges were added to the coin's rim. If a coin's edge was cut away, the telltale ridges would be lost.

In this problem, we'll use those ridges to prevent the coins from slipping. Consider two dimes within a track formed by parallel chopsticks. Although the coins can move, their snug fit makes both coins move at the same time. Therefore, if we were to rotate one of the dimes, the other would spin at the same speed but in the opposite direction. This results in both dimes moving along the track and maintaining their relative head-to-head position. Suppose, however, we change our setup and replace one of the dimes with a quarter. If the quarter is rotated along the track, how would its head-to-head position with the smaller dime change?

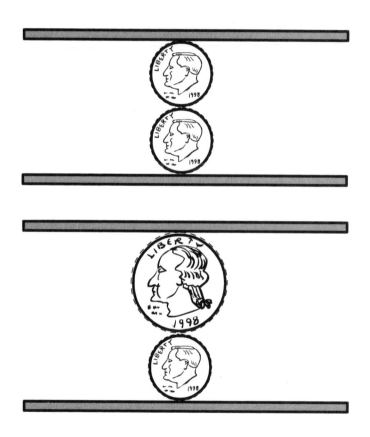

Answer on page 73.

More Coinage

◆ ◆ ◆

The four coins are positioned at the corners of a square. The side length of this square (measured from the center of each coin) is 8 inches. Here's the challenge. Can you change the positions of only two coins so that so that the new square formed by the coin arrangement has a side length slightly more than 5½ inches?

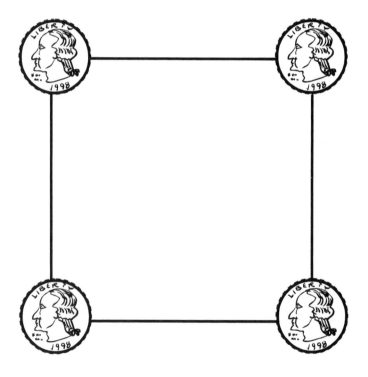

Answer on page 82.

Some Things Never Change

✦ ✦ ✦

People have written down puzzles for nearly 5000 years. One of the first puzzle collections was recorded about 1650 B.C. on a scroll called the Rhind papyrus. The word *Rhind* comes from the name Henry Rhind, a Scottish archaeologist who explored Egypt. *Papyrus* is a paper-like material that was used as a writing tablet by the ancient Egyptians.

The Rhind papyrus is a scroll that is over 18 feet long and about a foot wide. It was written on both sides by a person named Ahmes. Roughly translated (and somewhat updated), one of the puzzles from the scroll is presented below.

There are seven houses, each containing seven cats. Each cat kills seven mice, and each mouse would have eaten seven ears of corn. Each ear of corn would have produced seven sacks of grain. What is the total number of all of these items?

Answer on page 88.

Doing Wheelies

✦ ✦ ✦

The outer rim of each "double wheel" is twice the diameter of the wheel's inner rim. Suppose the top wheel rotates at ten revolutions per second. At what speed will wheel A and wheel B spin?

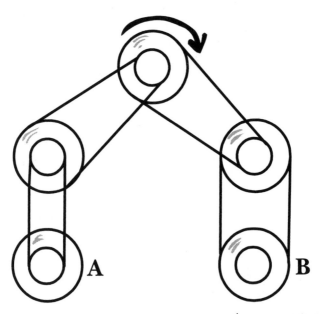

Answer on page 74.

More Wheelies

✦ ✦ ✦

The outermost rim of these wheels is twice the diameter of the middle rim. The middle rim is twice the diameter of the innermost rim. Suppose wheel A rotates at sixteen revolutions per second. How many revolutions will wheel C complete in a minute?

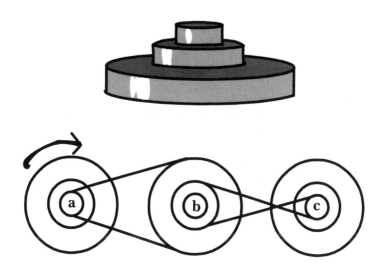

Answer on page 82–83.

Good Guess

✦ ✦ ✦

In order to win a free visit to the dentist, students had to guess the exact number of gumballs in a fish bowl. The students guessed 45, 41, 55, 50, and 43, but no one won. The guesses were off by 3, 7, 5, 7, and 2 (in no given order). From this information, determine the number of gumballs in the bowl.

Answer on page 76.

Check It Out

♦ ♦ ♦

The six sections below are parts of a 5 × 5 checkerboard grid. Can you piece them back together to form the original pattern?

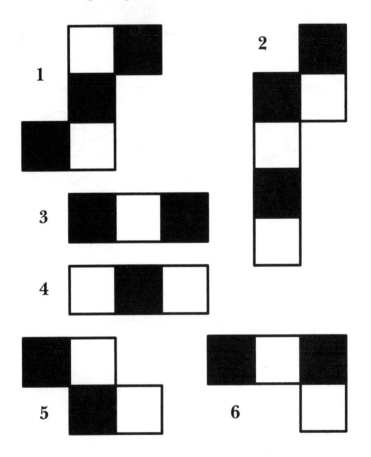

Answer on page 72.

Oops, I Wasn't Concentrating

✦ ✦ ✦

A pitcher is filled to the brim with grape juice. While raiding the refrigerator, Anthony accidentally knocks the pitcher over so that half of the contents spill out. Hoping no one will notice, Anthony adds tap water to the half-filled pitcher, bringing the volume of the diluted juice to the top. He then pours himself a glass of the watered down juice, leaving the pitcher three-fourths full.

"Yuck! This needs more flavor!" he exclaims and then adds more grape flavor by filling the pitcher to the brim with double-strength grape juice.

How does the concentration of this final solution compare with the original grape drink?

Answer on page 85.

Trying Times

✦ ✦ ✦

The triangle below is divided into four equal parts. Suppose you can paint one or more of these four smaller parts black. How many different and distinguishable patterns (including the pattern which has no painted triangles) can you form?

Remember, each pattern must be unique and not be duplicated by simply rotating the large figure.

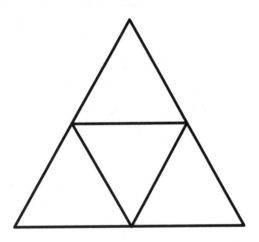

Answer on page 92.

Bridge, Anyone?

✦ ✦ ✦

Ever heard of Galloping Girdie? If not, perhaps you've seen an old science fiction movie that showed a clip of a large suspension bridge twisting apart and falling into the river below it. That was Galloping Girdie.

It spanned a large river in the state of Washington. Soon after it was constructed, people noticed that winds would cause the bridge to sway and shake. During one incident of heavy winds, the bridge shook so violently that it fell apart into the river below. Bye-bye, Girdie.

Now, it's your turn to design a bridge. To build it, you'll need three ice cream sticks. If you don't have these sticks, you can use three pieces of stiff cardboard. The cardboard sections should be 4½ inches long and ½ inch wide.

Position three cups in a triangular pattern. The cups should be placed so that the edge-to-edge distance between any two of the cups is 5 inches.

Hmm... 5-inch canyons, but only 4½-inch bridges. Your job is to construct a bridge using these three pieces and span the gaps connecting all three cups.

Answer on page 71.

Face Lift

Take a look at the shape below. Although it is made up of four identical cubes, you can only see three of them. The fourth cube is hidden in the bottom back-corner. Imagine picking the shape up and examining it from all angles. How many different cube faces can you count?

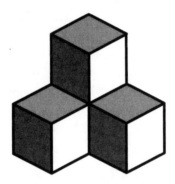

Okay, so it wasn't that hard. Try this one. The "double L" shape is made up of six cubes. The sixth cube is hidden in the back of the middle layer. If you could examine the stack from all angles, how many faces would you see?

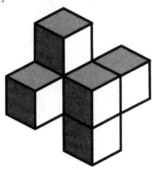

Okay, okay, okay. Here's one more. This one consists of only five cubes. Actually it resembles the "double L" shape, except that one of the cubes is removed.

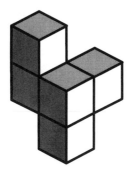

Answer on page 75.

Weighty Problem

✦ ✦ ✦

Did you know that during periods of weightlessness, astronauts lose bone mass? To prevent any serious loss, people in space must exercise. Stressing and stretching body parts help keep bone material from being reabsorbed into the body.

For a moment, let's imagine our weightless astronaut returning to Earth. She steps onto a scale and weighs herself. When the lab assistant asks her for her weight, she offers an obscure (but challenging) answer.

"According to this scale, I weigh 60 pounds plus half my weight."

Can you figure out how much this puzzling space traveler weighs?

Answer on pages 92–93.

Number Blocks

✦ ✦ ✦

Take a look at the three stacks of numbered blocks below. Can you rearrange the blocks by exchanging one (and *only* one) from each of the three stacks so that the sum of the numbers in each stack is equal to the sum of numbers in either other stack?

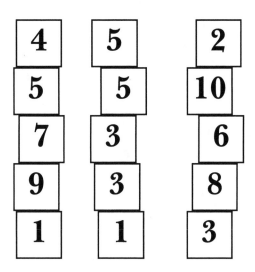

Answer on page 83.

Give Me Five

✦ ✦ ✦

How many 5's are in the number 5555?

Answer on page 76.

Separation Anxiety

◆ ◆ ◆

Using three straight lines, separate the apples from the oranges.

Answer on page 87.

Breaking Up Is Hard to Do... Sometimes

✦ ✦ ✦

Take a look at the square and triangle below. Both figures are divided into four equal and identical parts so that each part has the same shape of the original figure (only smaller).

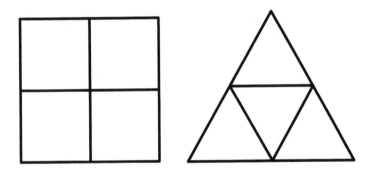

So far, so good. Now try to divide the figure below into four equal and identical parts, each with the same shape as the original figure.

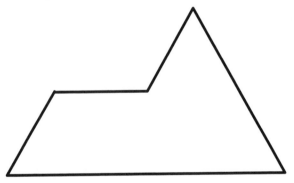

Answer on page 71.

Mind Slice

✦ ✦ ✦

Close your eyes and imagine a perfect sphere. Now, imagine a cleaver placed at a point anywhere on the surface of the sphere. How does changing the angle of the cleaver slice affect the *shape* of the exposed faces?

Answer on page 82.

Say Cheese

✦ ✦ ✦

The total surface area of any cube is equal to the sum of the surface areas of each of the six sides. For example, the cheese cube below measures 2 inches on each side. Therefore, the surface area of each side equals 2 inches × 2 inches, or 4 square inches. Since there are six sides, the total surface area of this cube is 24 square inches.

Now, the challenge. Using as many cuts as needed, divide this cube into pieces whose surface area sum is *twice* the surface area of this 2 × 2 cube.

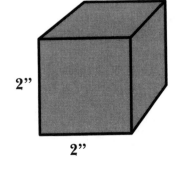

2"

2"

Answer on page 86.

Satellite Surveyor

✦ ✦ ✦

Satellites that orbit the Earth can see all sorts of things. Spy satellites, for example, have lenses that are powerful enough to "read" license plate numbers on cars. Other types of satellites can "look beneath" the Earth's surface. Some of these images have been used to uncover lost civilizations that have been buried for thousands of years under shifting desert sands.

In this problem, we'll use our satellite to help survey a plot of land.

The basic plot is a square that measures 20 miles on a side. Suppose the midpoint of each side is used as a marker to divide the entire plot into nine plots of various sizes and shapes. Without performing any higher math magic (just stick to plain ol' logic, with a little geometry), what is the area of the shaded central square?

NOTE: Before you bask in premature glory, it is not equal to 100 square miles!

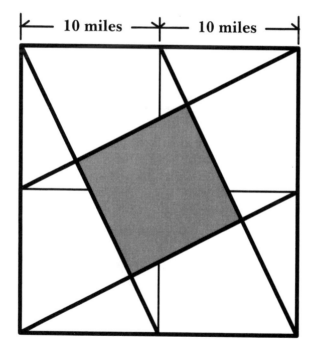

Answer on page 86.

Magic Star

✦ ✦ ✦

For those of you who are tired of magic squares and magic triangles, may we present *The Magic Star*? In this puzzle, you'll have to use the numbers one through twelve. Only one number can be placed in a circle, and all the numbers must be used. When placed correctly, the sum of all rows of four must be the same.

HINT: All of the side sums equal twenty-six.

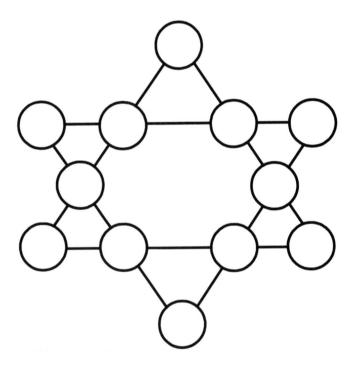

Answer on page 79.

Keep on Tickin'

♦ ♦ ♦

Divide the face of a watch into three sections. The sum of the numbers included on each section must equal the sum of the numbers on either of the other two sections. Let's not waste any time—the clock is ticking.

Answer on pages 77–78.

Cards, Anyone?

✦ ✦ ✦

Use a pair of scissors to carefully cut out two unequal corners of an index card as shown below. Can you now use the scissors to cut this modified card into two identical halves?

NOTE: The identical halves must be formed without flipping either piece over.

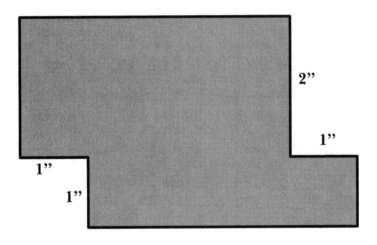

Let's keep up the cutting challenge. Copy the pattern below onto an index card. Use your scissors to trim off the excess card stock. Now, here's the challenge. Divide this shape into four equal and identical parts that can fit back together to form a perfect square.

Answers on page 72.

Going Batty

✦ ✦ ✦

Click, click, click, click. Like submarines, bats have a sonar system called echolocation. They use their echolocation to find objects. The clicking sounds made by bats move outward like the beam of a lighthouse. When the sounds strike an object (such as an insect meal), they are reflected back to the bat's large ears. With incredible speed, the bat's brain analyzes the echo return time and uses it to accurately locate the target's position.

Now, let's put that echolocation to work. Over a five-night period, a bat targets and captures a total of a hundred beetles. During each night, the bat captured six more beetles than on the previous night. How many beetles did the bat catch on each night?

Answer on page 76.

Sequence Grid

✦ ✦ ✦

A sequence grid is formed by items that are related by their order. Here are two examples. As you can see, the placement of the numbers and letters reflects a sequence.

512	256	128
64	32	16
8	4	2

A	C	E
G	I	K
M	O	Q

The first square is filled in an order based on dividing a number in half. The second square illustrates a sequence of letters that is separated by single (but not recorded) middle letters.

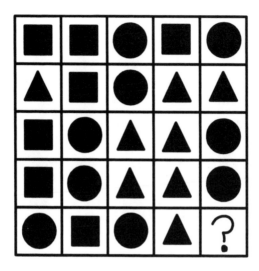

Now that you know what a sequence grid is, here's one to sharpen your puzzling skills on.

Answer on page 88.

Breaking the Rules

◆ ◆ ◆

A ruler is placed on two pieces of chalk as shown below. As the ruler is pushed, it moves 4 inches ahead. How far did either one of the chalk pieces roll?

Answer on page 71.

Balance

Suppose you have a balance and a 2-gram and 5-gram mass. How can the balance be used only three times to separate 80 grams of fat into piles of 13 grams and 67 grams?

Answer on page 70.

Big Magic

The figure below is called a magic square. Do you see why it's called magic? The sum of any three-box side (and the two three-box diagonals) is equal to the sum of any other side (or diagonal). In this case, they are all equal to fifteen.

8	3	4
1	5	9
6	7	2

The sections belong to a four-by-four magic square. Your job is to assemble these sections into a complete sixteen-box magic square. To do so, you'll *first* have to uncover the sum of the side for this figure.

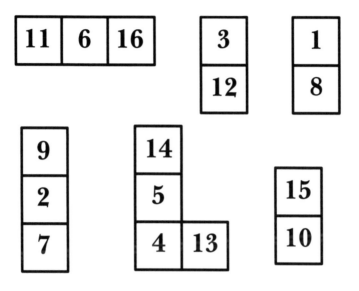

Answer on page 70.

Togetherness

✦ ✦ ✦

A computer and its monitor weigh a total of 48 pounds. If the monitor weighs twice as much as the computer, how much does each piece of hardware weigh?

Answer on page 91.

Look Over Here

✦ ✦ ✦

Note the direction in which each eye looks. Can you uncover the pattern? Good. Now find the empty eye. In which direction should this eye be looking?

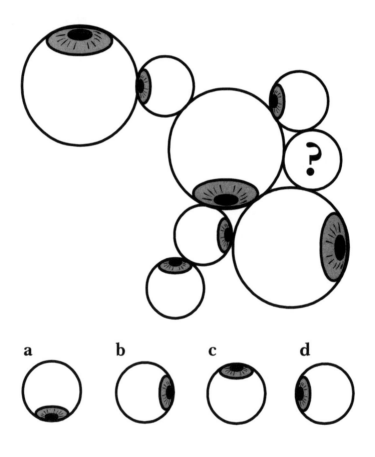

a   **b**   **c**   **d**

Answer on page 79.

Time on Your Hands

✦ ✦ ✦

Examine the series of three clock-faces shown below. When you uncover the pattern of the hand movement, select from the choice of times that will be closest to what the fourth clock should read.

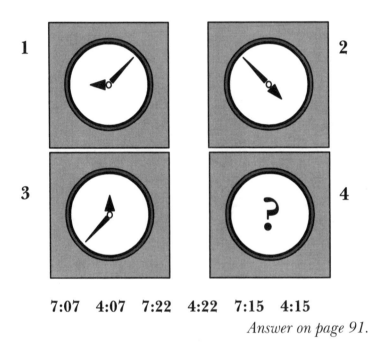

7:07   4:07   7:22   4:22   7:15   4:15

Answer on page 91.

Take Your Pick

✦ ✦ ✦

Arrange eight toothpicks (on a flat surface) so that they form two squares and four triangles.

Answer on page 90.

One Way Only

✦ ✦ ✦

Can you trace the following figure using only one continuous line? Place your pencil anywhere on the figure. Then, draw the rest of the figure without lifting your pencil from the page.

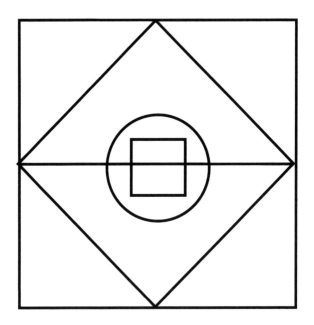

NOTE: This line cannot cross over itself nor retrace any part of its path.

Answer on page 83.

Lasagna Cut

A square pan filled with piping-hot lasagna is set aside to cool. When the hungry chefs return, they discover that a quarter of the lasagna has mysteriously disappeared (as shown below). Frustrated, they decide to divide the remaining piece into four equal portions before any more is eaten. All cuts must be normal—no slicing through the plane of the surface allowed. What is the cutting pattern that will meet the needs of these chefs?

HINT: The simplest solution requires cutting this meal into eight pieces and supplying each person with two smaller pieces.

Answer on pages 78–79.

Iron Horse Race

✦ ✦ ✦

Two trains race against each other on parallel tracks. *The Casey Jones Special* is a coal-fed steam engine that travels at a respectable speed. The newer, oil-burning *Metropolitan Diesel* travels 1½ times the speed of *The Casey Jones Special*. To make the race a closer competition, *The Casey Jones Special* begins the race 1½ hours before its opponent. How long will it take the *Metropolitan Diesel* to catch up to the slower steam engine?

Answer on page 77.

Thick as a Brick

♦ ♦ ♦

If the chimney below is complete on all four sides, how many bricks does the whole structure contain?

Answer on page 91.

Here, Art, Art, Art

✦ ✦ ✦

How quickly can you uncover the perfect five-pointed star hidden in the design below?

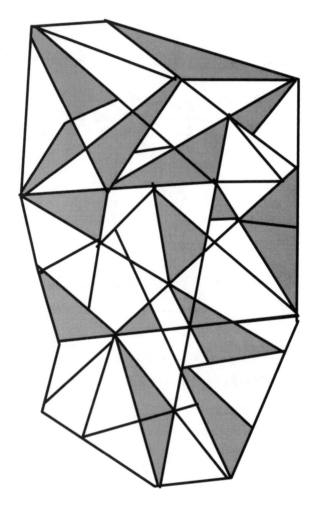

Answer on page 76.

Surrounded By Squares

How many squares can you uncover in the pattern below? Don't forget to count the outer border as one of your answers!

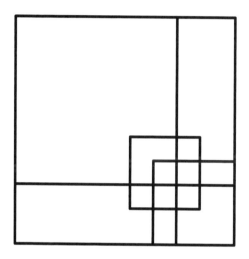

Answer on page 90.

More Cheese

✦ ✦ ✦

A grocer has a large cube of cheese that she wishes to divide into twenty-seven smaller and equal-sized cubes. To cut out the twenty-seven blocks, she uses two cuts to divide the cube into three slices. She stacks these slices atop of each other and makes two more cuts. Finally, she rotates the cube a quarter-turn and makes the final cut. The result is twenty-seven identical cubes made with six cuts. Is it possible to get the twenty-seven cubes with fewer cuts? If so, how?

Answer on page 81.

Break It Up!

If you look carefully, you'll be able to uncover thirty squares in the toothpick pattern below. Your challenge is to find the fewest number of toothpicks that, when removed, leaves no complete square pattern intact.

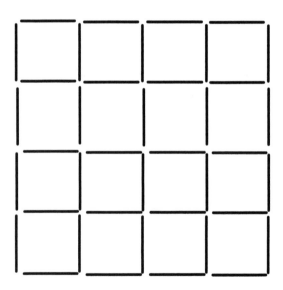

Answer on page 70.

Exactly... Well, Almost

♦ ♦ ♦

Which of the designs below is unlike the other five?

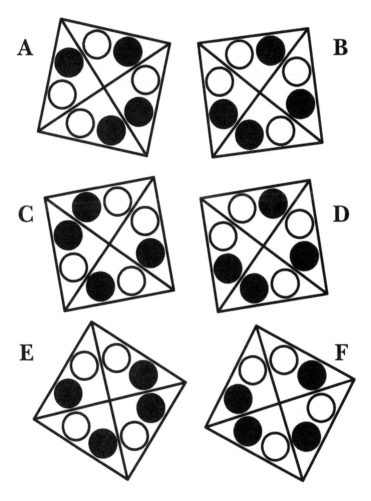

Answer on page 75.

Parts of a Whole

♦ ♦ ♦

Copy the five shapes shown below onto a separate sheet of paper. Use a pair of scissors to carefully cut out the shapes. Here's the challenge. Arrange them to form a triangle whose three sides are of equal length.

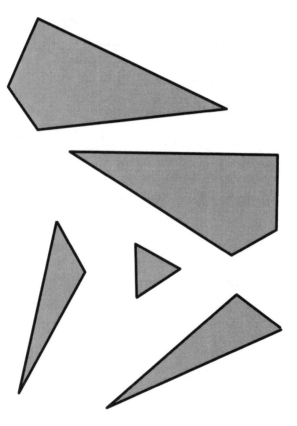

Answer on page 84.

A Game for Losers

✦ ✦ ✦

The object of this modified game of tic-tac-toe is to lose! In order to win, you must force your opponent to complete three squares in a row. Let's enter a game that has already been started. You are "O" and it is your turn. In which box or boxes should you place your "O" marker to ensure that you win by losing (no matter where your opponent goes)?

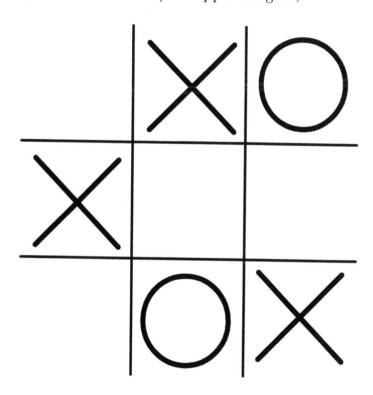

Answer on page 75.

Roller Coaster, Roll!

✦ ✦ ✦

Ed and his identical twin brother Ed build roller coaster tracks. They've just completed two hills that are both 40 feet high. As you can see, the slopes of the two hills are somewhat different. Ed (the older twin) rides a car that will travel along on a straight slope. Ed (the younger twin) rides a car that will travel along a curved slope.

If both cars are released at the exact same time, which Ed will arrive at the bottom of this slope first?

Answer on page 86.

Sum Puzzle

✦ ✦ ✦

Copy the pattern and numbers shown below onto a sheet of paper. Then carefully use a pair of scissors to separate the sheet into nine separate squares. Rebuild the larger square using the following strategy. The sum of any two adjacent numbers must equal ten. Have fun.

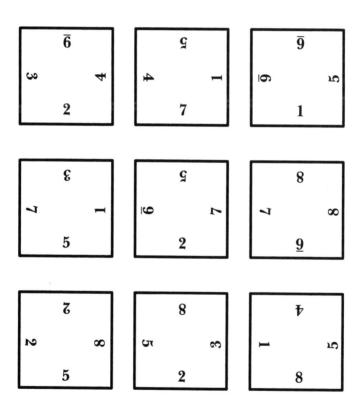

Answer on page 89.

A Class Act

✦ ✦ ✦

There are thirty students in a class. Five of these students do not play any sort of musical instrument. Among the others, eighteen students play guitar. Six of these guitar players also play keyboards. How many of students in the class play only keyboards?

Answer on page 73.

Cool Cut

✦ ✦ ✦

Shut your eyes and try to imagine a perfect ice cube. If you're good at visualizing, you may be able to "see" the edges and faces that are positioned on the far side of the cube. Good. Now, here's the challenge.

With one cut, how can you divide this cube so that a perfect triangular face is exposed? Don't forget, a regular triangle has all three sides of equal length.

WATCH IT. YOUR IMAGINATION IS LEAKING ONTO THE TABLE.

Answer on page 74.

Melt Down

✦ ✦ ✦

Unlike most liquids, water freezes into a solid that is less dense than its former liquid state. Since it is less dense, ice floats in water. At the surface, the ice acts as an insulator to help trap heat within the water below. This layer of frozen insulation actually insulates lakes, rivers, ponds, and oceans from freezing into a complete solid.

Now let's bring this information back to the kitchen. An ice cube floats freely in a glass filled to the brim with water. Will the water level rise or sink as the ice cube melts?

Answer on page 80.

What's the Angle?

✦ ✦ ✦

An equilateral triangle has three sides that are all of equal length. This familiar shape can be constructed from three identical pieces. Examine the shapes below. Which of these shapes illustrates this building block? Once you've selected the shape, make three copies of it on a separate sheet of paper. Cut out and arrange these pieces so that they form an equilateral triangle.

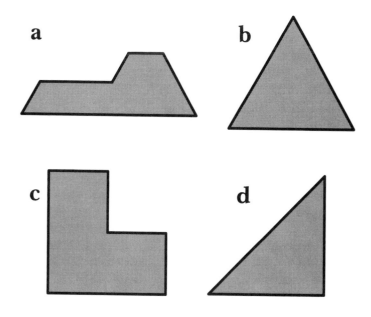

a

b

c

d

Answer on page 93.

Here, Spot, Spot, Spot

✦ ✦ ✦

Without lifting your pencil from the paper, draw six straight lines that connect all sixteen of the dots below. To make things more of a challenge, the line pattern that you create must begin at the "x".

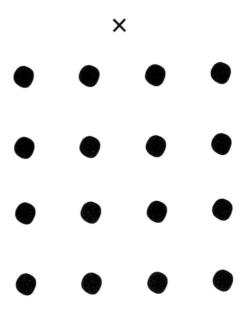

Answer on page 77.

Keeping Time

✦ ✦ ✦

The strike of a lightning bolt can create a tremendous surge of electricity. If this electric flow reaches the delicate circuits of a computer, it can "burn out" the sensitive components. To prevent against this damage, computers are plugged into surge protectors, which stop the electric flow if a damaging level of electricity is detected.

In this problem, there are no surge protectors. Two electronic clocks are plugged directly into the wall socket. A surge of electricity flows through both clocks and affects their time-keeping circuits. One clock is now 5 minutes per hour fast. The other clock is now 5 minutes per hour slow. In how many hours will the clocks be exactly one hour apart?

Answer on page 78.

Wrap It Up

✦ ✦ ✦

You will soon engage your intellect in this book's final critical thinking puzzle.

Did you know that fortune cookies didn't originate in China? They were created in the U.S. by the owner of an Asian restaurant who wished to amuse his customers while they waited for their meals to be cooked. Over time, fortune cookies evolved into a treat that is now offered at the end of the meal. That's a wrap. And speaking of wraps...

Take a look at the steps in which the cookie wrapper below was folded. In the final step, two holes were punched through the layers of the folds.

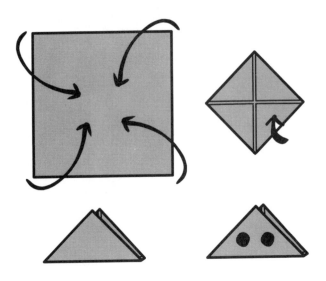

Now unroll this wrapper. Which of the patterns would it resemble?

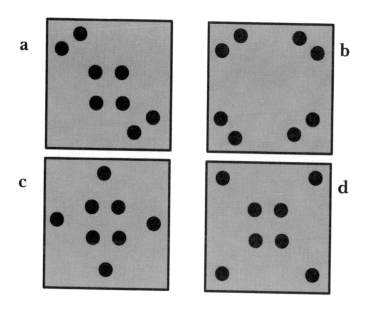

Answer on page 94.

ANSWERS

Balance

First, use the balance to divide the 80 grams into two piles of 40 grams. Then divide one of the 40-gram piles in half. Now balance the 20 grams against the 7 grams produced by the two masses. The 13 grams that are removed from the balance form one pile. The 7 grams added to the 40 grams + 20 grams produces the larger pile of 67 grams.

Big Magic

The sum of the side is thirty-four, and the square looks like this:

1	11	6	16
8	14	3	9
15	5	12	2
10	4	13	7

Break It Up!

Nine toothpicks need to be removed as shown below.

Breaking the Rules

Two inches. Each chalk piece will advance only half the distance covered by the ruler.

Breaking Up Is Hard to Do...
Sometimes

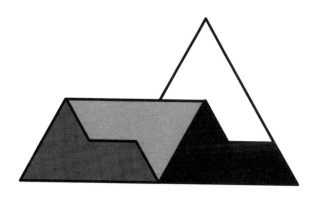

Bridge, Anyone?

The sticks below are arranged so that they support each other in a central triangle formed by over- and underlapping supports.

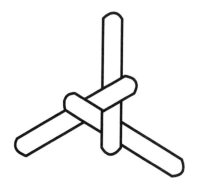

Cards, Anyone?

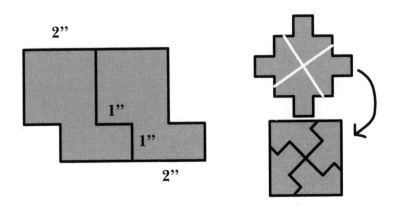

Change of Pace

a. either 5 pennies ($.05) + 4 nickels ($.20) + 1 quarter ($.25) = $.50; or 10 nickels ($.05) = $.50

b. 25 pennies ($.25) + 1 nickel ($.05) + 2 dimes ($.20) + 2 quarters ($.50) = $1.00

Check It Out

		4		
	1		2	
	5			
				3
6				

A Class Act

Seven students play only keyboards. A diagram helps illustrate and solve this problem.

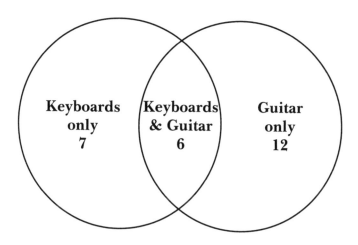

Coin Roll

The coins maintain their relative position to each other as they move along the track. What changes is the direction in which the coin images point.

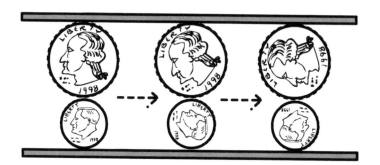

Cool Cut

Make the cut from one corner straight across to the corners as shown below. Each side of this regular triangle that is formed is equal in length to the diagonal of the square.

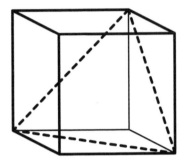

Doing Wheelies

Wheel A would be spinning at five revolutions per minute. Wheel B would be spinning at twenty revolutions per minute. The difference in speed results from the "gearing up" and the "gearing down" from the first wheel set to the second wheel set. The belts between the second and third wheel sets do not affect the spin.

Don't Stop Now

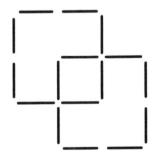

Exactly... Well, Almost

E. It is the mirror image of the other repeating (but rotating) design.

Face Lift

a. Eighteen faces.

b. Twenty-six faces.

c. Twenty-two faces.

A Game for Losers

By placing your "O" marker in either of the boxes indicated below, you are ensured a victory no matter where your opponent places his or her "X"s.

Get Set. Go!

150 miles long. In order to complete 30 miles of distance, the faster cyclist requires 1 hour of time while the slower cyclist needs 1.20 hours. Therefore, the time difference

per 30 miles of travel is .20 hours. In order to increase the difference to 1 hour, multiple the 30 miles by 5.

Give Me Five

1111. Easy, unless of course you forget all it takes to solve this problem is to divide 5555 by 5!

Going Batty

The number of beetles captured on each successive night were 8, 14, 20, 26, and 32.

Good Guess

Forty-eight gumballs. Since two guesses were off by seven and no guesses were repeated, these values had to refer to numbers at the opposite extremes of the spread. The two extremes are 41 and 55. If you add 7 to one and take 7 away from the other, you arrive at the middle number of 48.

Here, Art, Art, Art

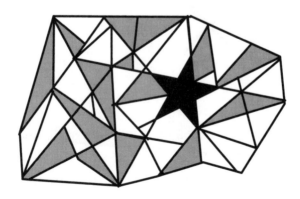

Here, Spot, Spot, Spot

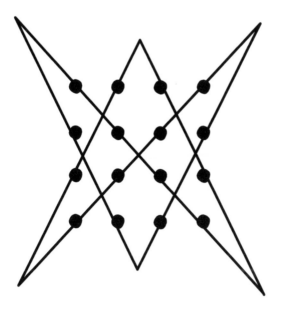

Iron Horse Race

The trains will be tied 3 hours after the faster train (or 4½ hours after the slower train) begins the race. For example, if the trains travel 60 mph and 90 mph, the 4½-hour journey for the slower train covers 270 miles, while the 3-hour journey for the faster train also covers 270 miles.

Keep On Tickin'

First you'll need to find out what each section needs to add to. To get this number, add up every number on the clock's face (1 + 2 + 3 + 4 + 5 + 6 + 7 + 8 + 9 + 10 + 11 + 12 = 78). Divide 78 by 3 and you'll get 26—the sum that each section must add to. The next part is relatively easy, since the numbers are already laid out in a ready-to-add pattern.

Keeping Time

Six hours. In 6 hours, the slow clock will be exactly 30 minutes behind while the fast clock will be exactly 30 minutes ahead of time.

Lasagna Cut

Each person gets one large and one small triangular piece.

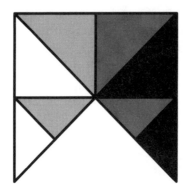

Here's a slightly different pattern that produces four similar-shaped slices (if we assume the connecting points between the triangle pairs remain uncut).

Look Over Here

b The direction of the look is based upon the number of neighboring eyes that are in contact with the eye's circumference. Eyes that "touch" three other circles (such as the circle in question) have a pupil that points to the right.

Magic Star

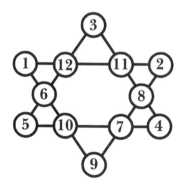

Main Attraction

Take either bar (it doesn't matter which one) and touch one end of the bar to the middle of the other bar. If the bar you are holding is a magnet, then its pole will cause the nonmagnetized bar to move. If, however, you've picked up the nonmagnetized bar, no attraction will occur. That's because neither of the poles is being touched.

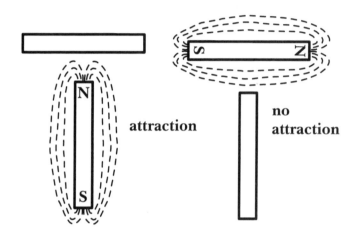

attraction

no attraction

Melt Down

The level of water will not change. Although the top of the cube floats above the surface of the water, the amount of water in the entire ice cube can fill a space equal to the dimensions occupied by the part of the cube that is under the water's surface. In other words, as the ice cube turns to water, it produces the same amount of water as the space occupied by the submerged part of the cube.

Mind Bend

Place three parallel cuts in the card. Two of the cuts should be positioned on one side, while a single central cut should be made on the opposite side (as shown below). Then place a twist in the card so that half of the upper surface is formed by the "bottom-side" of the card. For extra fun, you might want to tape the folded card by all of its edges to the desk (making it more difficult to uncover the baffling "twist").

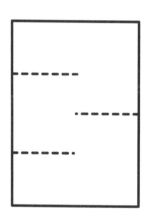 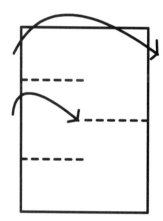

More Cheese

No. Six cuts are the fewest number of cuts needed to produce the twenty-seven smaller cubes. Stacking doesn't result in fewer cuts. Think of it this way: that innermost cube of the twenty-seven must be formed by a cut on each of its six sides.

Mind Slice

The angle of the cut will not affect the shape at all. All cuts will produce faces that are perfect circles. The feature that does change with the cutting angle is the circle size.

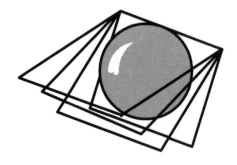

More Coinage

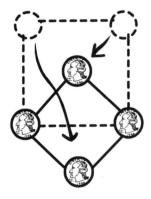

More Wheelies

480 revolutions. Since wheel B's rim is four times longer than wheel A's rim, it spins at one-fourth the speed (4 rps). Likewise, wheel B's rim is twice as long as wheel C's rim.

Therefore, wheel C's rim spins twice as fast (8 rps). In 1 minute, C wheel will complete 60 × 8 revolutions, or 480 revolutions.

Number Blocks

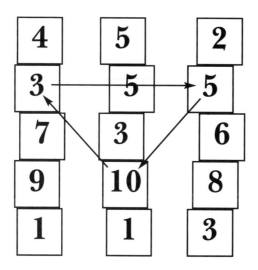

One Way Only

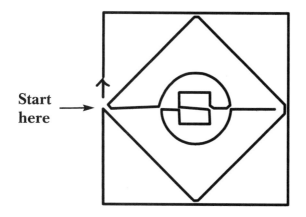

Start here

Parts of a Whole

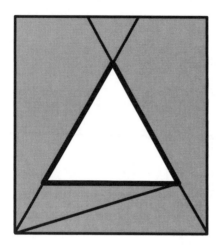

Puzzle Paths

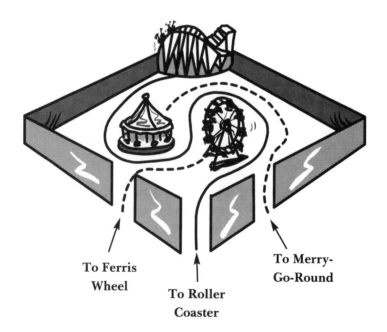

To Ferris
Wheel

To Roller
Coaster

To Merry-
Go-Round

Oops, I Wasn't Concentrating

It is weaker than the original solution. In order have the original concentration, Anthony would have to add grape juice that is 2½ times the regular strength.

Raises and Cuts

They are now both earning the exact same amount. To prove this, let's take a sample first-week salary of $100 for both Moe and Bo. After the first adjustment, Moe earned $110 while Bo earned $90. During the second adjustment, Moe was cut by $11 to $99. At the same time, Bo was increased by $9 to $99.

Runaway Runway

Six intersections as shown below.

Roller Coaster Roll

Young Ed. The car that travels along the curved slope accelerates faster. This extra speed results from the quick drop in the path that allows the car to quickly pick up speed as the car moving down the straight slope accelerates at a slower and more uniform rate.

Satellite Surveyor

80 square miles. If you examine the dissected grid, you'll uncover that the composite shapes include side-by-side pairs that can be joined to form four squares. The total area is 20 × 20, or 400 square miles. Each of the five identical squares contains one-fifth, or 80 square miles.

Say Cheese

Make three cuts that divide the cube into eight smaller but equal cubes. Each of these eight cubes has a side length of 1 inch to produce a surface area of 6 square inches. The sum of the eight cube surface areas is 48 square inches.

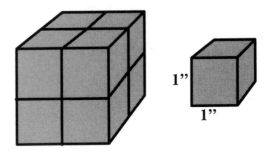

Screws in the Head

As the threads turn, they will produce a counterclockwise motion in the gear of the tuning post. This motion will decrease the tension in the string to produce a note of lower pitch.

Screwy Stuff

The threads of screw A form a spiral that would "go into" the wood block. In contrast, the opposite spiral of screw B would result in this screw moving out of the wooden block.

Separation Anxiety

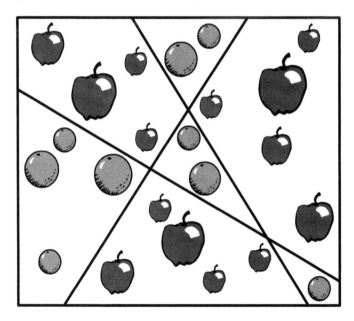

Sequence Grid

Triangle. The grid is filled by a series of number sequences. The first sequence consists of only one member—a square. The second and adjoining sequence includes a square + circle. The third sequence expands to include a square + circle + triangle. The complete sequence from which the "?" can be determined is square + circle + triangle + triangle + circle + circle.

Some Things Never Change

$7 + 49 + 343 + 2401 + 16,807 = 19,607$.

Spiral^2

The complete path from entrance to center is 5000 feet. To obtain this distance, determine the total area of the structure (10,000 square feet). Now mentally unroll the spiral. Divide the 10,000-square-foot area by the area associated with one foot of forward travel. Since the corridor is 2 feet wide, the area for a single foot of forward motion is 2 square feet. Dividing 10,000 by 2, we arrive at the total distance of 5000 feet.

The Race Is On

The wheel with the centrally placed lead will accelerate fastest. This behavior reflects a property of physics that ice skaters execute during their moves. As a skater spins, the speed of the spin can be adjusted by altering his or her distribution of weight. As the arms extend, the spinning skater slows. As the arms draw in, the spin accelerates.

Sum Puzzle

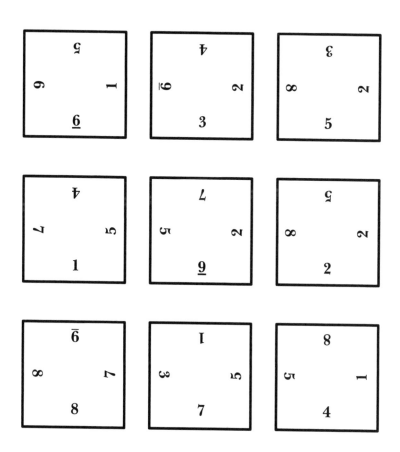

Surrounded By Squares

Thirteen squares.

Take 'em Away

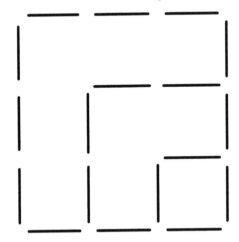

Take Your Pick

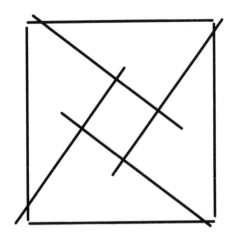

Thick as a Brick

Sixty bricks. You don't have to count all of the bricks. Just count the bricks in the uppermost layer (twelve) and multiply by the number of layers (five) so that you arrive at a total number of sixty bricks.

Time on Your Hands

7:22. For each given time, the minute hand advances a quarter of a complete counterclockwise rotation, while the hour hand advances three-eighths of a complete counterclockwise rotation. The final arrangement looks like this:

Togetherness

The computer weighs 16 pounds and its monitor weighs 32 pounds.

Trying Times

Eight unique triangles as shown below.

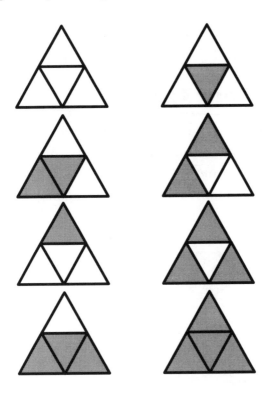

Turn, Turn, Turn

F.

Weighty Problem

120 pounds. If she needs to add "half of her weight" to get her full weight, then the weight that she does tell (60 pounds) must be half of her total. Therefore, 60 pounds is

half of her weight. 60 + 60 = 120 pounds. If this doesn't seem right, just work it backwards starting with the 120 pounds.

What's the Angle?

a. Three copies of this shape are positioned as shown here.

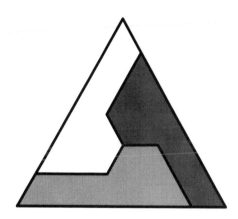

Whale of a Problem

Two minutes. The amount of time needed to catch the seals doesn't change. Since two whales can catch two seals in 2 minutes, it is logical to assume that a single whale can catch one seal in that same period of time. Likewise, three whales can catch three seals in 2 minutes. As long as the number of whales is equal to the number of seals, the time doesn't change. Therefore, ten killer whales will also take 2 minutes to catch ten seals.

Wrap It Up

d. Here's what you see as you unwrap the folds.

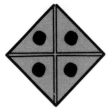

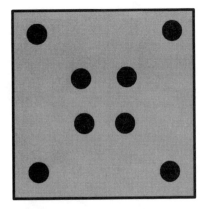

INDEX

Page key: puzzle, *answer*.

About the Author

MICHAEL DISPEZIO has always had a fondness for integrating learning with creativity, critical thinking, and performance. After tiring of "counting hairs on copepods," Michael traded the marine science laboratory for the classroom. Over the years, he has taught physics, chemistry, mathematics, and rock 'n' roll musical theater. During his classroom years, Michael co-authored a chemistry book, which launched his writing career.

To date, Michael is the author of *Critical Thinking Puzzles, Great Critical Thinking Puzzles,* and *Visual Thinking Puzzles* (all from Sterling) as well as eighteen science textbooks, a producer of several educational videos, and a creator of hundreds of supplementary products and science education articles. His most recent science education project was authoring *The Science of HIV,* a teaching package published by the National Association of Science Teachers.

Michael's expertise in both video and science education has resulted in several trips to train counterparts in the Middle East. When he isn't presenting workshops for science teachers, Michael is at home writing, creating, and puzzle solving.